The Quiz Book

Clues to You & Your Friends, Too!

By Laura Allen

Illustrated by Debbie Tilley

American Girl™

Dear Reader,

Are you a **happy camper?** How **silly** are you? Can you keep a **secret?** Find out by taking **quizzes** that reveal these and many more clues about you.

You'll **discover** who you are today and who you may become in the future. Just remember that as you grow, your **feelings** and **thoughts** change, too. Your answers today may be different tomorrow!

So sharpen your pencil and gather friends and family around. Get set to **learn** a little—and **laugh** a lot!

Your friends at American Girl

Contents

What's Your Style? **5**

Are You a Snoop? **8**

Tickled Pink or Feeling Blue? **11**

Show Time! **13**

S.S. Friendship **15**

Are You a Happy Camper? **17**

How Do You Doodle? **21**

Tidy Test **26**

Are You Too Nice? **29**

Good Cents **32**

Silly Scale **35**

Do You Dare? **38**

Pal Poll **40**

Pssst! **44**

Are You a Class Act? **47**

Moment of Truth **50**

Friendship Rings **53**

Losing Your Cool **58**

Can You Read Minds? **61**

The Write Clues **62**

Parent Poll **66**

Are You Ready for a Pet? **70**

Food for Thought **73**

Starring You! **76**

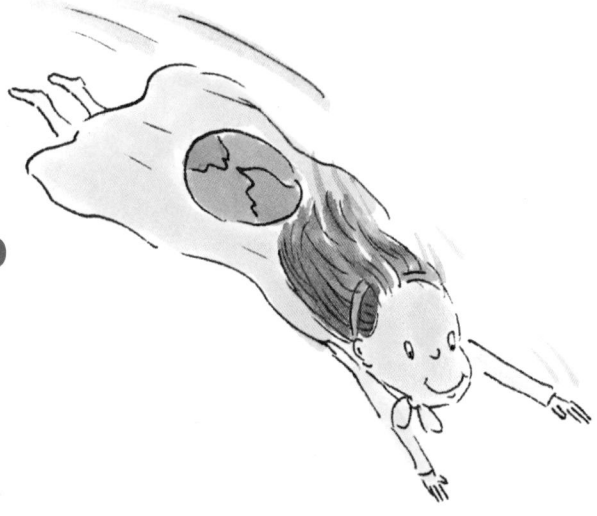

What's Your Style?

Are you **easygoing**, **soft** and **sweet**, or **bold** and **trendy**?
Circle the letter next to the answer that describes you best.

1. If you could buy a new beach towel, it would most likely have . . .

a. your favorite team's logo.

b. a colorful floral pattern.

c. big, bold stripes or shapes.

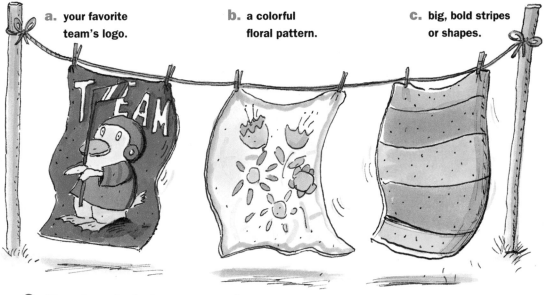

2. Your favorite hair accessory is . . .

a. a hairbrush.

b. a velvet headband.

c. a butterfly clip.

3. Of these bracelets, your favorite would be . . .

a. a friendship bracelet your best friend made for you.

b. a charm bracelet.

c. a silver chain with beads that you added yourself.

4. The hairstyle you like best is . . .

a. short and easy.

b. French braids.

c. the same cut that my favorite TV star has.

5. Your favorite hat is . . .

a. a baseball cap.　　**b.** a straw sun hat.　　**c.** a floppy black velvet hat.

6. If you were invited to a costume party, you'd most likely go as . . .

a. a cowgirl.　　**b.** a medieval princess.　　**c.** a hippie.

7. Your favorite shoes are . . .

a. sneakers.

b. strappy sandals.

c. black oxfords with chunky soles.

8. You sleep in . . .

a. a big T-shirt and sweatpants.

b. a nightgown.

c. PJ top and bottoms with a fun pattern.

Answers

Mostly **a**'s

You're into what is comfy, casual, or sporty. You have a breezy, easygoing style.

Mostly **b**'s

Pretty things make you smile. Your style is soft and sweet with a touch of glamour.

Mostly **c**'s

Bold and trendy describes your style. You're often the first to try out the latest look.

Are You a Snoop?

Does your **nose** go where it's not **supposed** to go?
Circle the letter next to the answer that fits you best.

1. While looking for a book at the library, you hear two classmates in the next row whispering. You keep very quiet and try to listen to what they're saying.

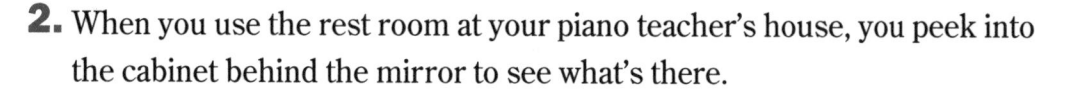

a. Yes, that's me.
b. I might do this.
c. I'd never do this.

2. When you use the rest room at your piano teacher's house, you peek into the cabinet behind the mirror to see what's there.

a. Yes, that's me.
b. I might do this.
c. I'd never do this.

3. While sharpening a pencil at your dad's desk at home, you see a letter to Aunt Doris on his computer screen. You read it.

a. Yes, that's me.
b. I might do this.
c. I'd never do this.

4. You're in the hall closet looking for a box to wrap your mom's holiday present in when you stumble on a huge shopping bag from Toy Town. You peek inside.

a. Yes, that's me.
b. I might do this.
c. I'd never do this.

5. Your sister accidentally left her diary sitting on top of her dresser—unlocked! So when she goes to band practice, you sneak a peek.

    a. Yes, that's me.
    b. I might do this.
    c. I'd never do this.

6. You're waiting at your teacher's desk to ask a question when you notice her grade book lying wide open. You read everyone's grades.

    a. Yes, that's me.
    b. I might do this.
    c. I'd never do this.

7. You see two girls passing a note in class and giggling. Later on, you see the note crumpled up in the garbage. You fish it out to read it.

    a. Yes, that's me.
    b. I might do this.
    c. I'd never do this.

8. A few days before your birthday, you hear your mother whispering on the phone. You quietly pick up the phone in another room to find out who's on the other end.

    a. Yes, that's me.
    b. I might do this.
    c. I'd never do this.

Answers

If you answered **a** more than once . . .

Too Snoopy

You may need to learn where to draw the line between what's your business and what isn't. Respecting other people's privacy is important, and it makes you someone they can trust. So before you let your curiosity get the best of you, stop and ask yourself, "Does this really concern me? Is this really something I *need* to know, or is this just something I *want* to know?"

Mostly **b**'s

Sometime Spy

You know it's not right to pry, but you just can't help yourself sometimes. Next time something private catches your eye, stop and listen to your conscience. Chances are that uneasiness you feel means you're sticking your nose where it doesn't belong.

Mostly **c**'s

Snoop Free

You don't let your eyes wander around to find gossip or to satisfy your curiosity. What's more, because others have learned that they can count on you to know what's your business and what's not, they respect you and often trust you with their secrets.

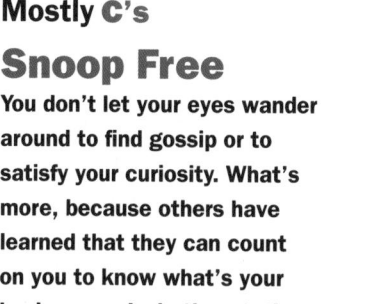
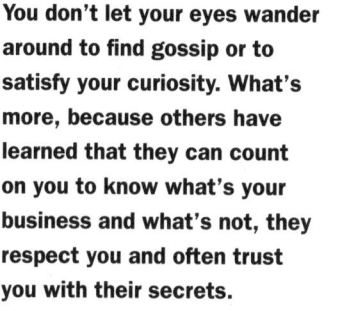

Tickled Pink or Feeling Blue?

Study the colors below and pick the one that you think matches your mood today. Then turn the page to see what some experts believe that color says about you.

Answers

Red

You're full of energy today. You're ready to go after a goal, ace a test, or just make each moment its best.

Yellow

You're feeling cheerful and bright. You may be looking ahead to future adventures or a fun escape.

Blue

You're in a thoughtful, mellow mood. You're seeking a quiet place to hang out in today.

Green

You're anxious and eager for others to recognize something special you've done.

Purple

Passionate and creative describes you right now. You're letting your heart rule your head.

Black

You're strong, determined, and perhaps a little reckless at heart today. You may even feel the need to make a change and give yourself a fresh start.

Pink

You're feeling kind and playful, spreading smiles and laughter wherever you go today.

Show Time!

Are you **on time** or **late for the show?** Circle the letter next to the answer that describes you best.

1. When it's time to get up for school, you . . .

   a. jump right out of bed.

   b. lie there for five more dreamy minutes, then get up.

   c. fall back asleep until Dad throws open the door to your room, opens the blinds, and yells, "Get up sleepyhead!"

2. As you get ready for school, you . . .

   a. keep a close eye on the time.

   b. glance at a clock once or twice.

   c. never check the time—Mom tells you when it's time to go.

3. Your watch is set . . .

   a. five minutes fast.

   b. on the dot.

   c. What watch?

4. When you arrive at the bus stop, you're . . .

   a. the first one there.

   b. right on time.

   c. the last one to show up.

5. You have a soccer game after school, so you . . .

   a. go straight to the soccer field from school. You want to practice before the others arrive.

   b. go straight home from school to get ready. You arrive at the field just in time for warm-up.

   c. go home after school to watch your favorite cartoon and get ready during commercials. When your show is over, you rush to the field in time for the first whistle.

6. At dinnertime, you . . .

a. are the first one to sit down at the table.

b. get there just as everyone else is sitting down.

c. usually hear someone shout, "Your food is getting cold!"

7. When a friend and her mom drive over to pick you up, you're . . .

a. ready and waiting on the front steps.

b. putting your coat on and peeking out the window as they pull up.

c. yelling, "Hey Mom! Where's my other shoe?"

8. When you go to see a movie, you . . .

a. get there early so you can sit anywhere.

b. arrive just in time to get a decent seat.

c. stumble around in the dark and end up sitting in the front row.

Answers

Mostly a's
Previews

You make it a point to be early. You don't want to miss out on anything—especially if you're competing for the best seat in the house!

Mostly b's
Show Time

Your mind tends to run like clockwork. You have a good sense of time and can get to where you're going without breaking a sweat.

Mostly c's
Excuse Me...

You probably lose track of time often. Try to plan ahead and keep your eye on the clock. And if your lateness just can't be helped, call ahead to let someone know.

S.S. Friendship

Can you steer clear of friendship trouble?
Take this quiz to find out.

1. You and Ali made plans to go to the library, but now Zoe asks you to go miniature golfing. You love mini golf, so you call Ali and tell her you're sick.

   a. Yes, that's me.   **b.** I might do this.   **c.** I'd never do this.

2. You get into an argument with your friend Lisa because you think she stole your best babysitting job. As long as you're arguing, you bring up the time she borrowed your barrette and "forgot" to return it.

   a. Yes, that's me.   **b.** I might do this.   **c.** I'd never do this.

3. At recess, your friend is wearing a new, super-insulated, bright-white winter coat. When a couple of classmates start teasing her and calling her a marshmallow, you can't resist joining in on the fun.

   a. Yes, that's me.   **b.** I might do this.   **c.** I'd never do this.

4. You and Dana have been friends forever. But when Dana's not around and your new friends make fun of her, you go along with them.

   a. Yes, that's me.   **b.** I might do this.   **c.** I'd never do this.

S. S. FRIENDSHIP

5. Your new friend has been hogging you. In fact, you can't do anything with anyone else without her expecting to be included. So you avoid her at school and tell your other friends to keep any plans you make with them a secret.

a. Yes, that's me.　　**b.** I might do this.　　**c.** I'd never do this.

6. Your two best friends have started doing things without you. First it was the movies, then the mall, now the skating rink. You want to ask why, but you're afraid they'll say they don't like you anymore. So you say nothing and wait it out.

a. Yes, that's me.　　**b.** I might do this.　　**c.** I'd never do this.

Answers

If you answered **a** or **b** more than once, you may need to learn how to keep your friendships out of icy waters.

1. Always stay true to your word and honor the first plan you made. When you start fibbing to a friend to take advantage of a better offer, you're headed for trouble!

2. Stick to the issue that upset you today. When you restart old arguments, you take everyone's attention away from what you need to talk about right now.

3. Teasing is usually only fun for the teaser. Joking about something that could embarrass a friend or hurt her feelings is downright cruel. Unless you want to spring a leak in a good friendship, don't do it.

4. Being two-faced can damage your friendship and your reputation. Be respectful of your friend's feelings whether she's present or not.

5. If you just avoid your friend, she's not going to get the right message. You need to tell her just how you feel: you value her friendship, but that doesn't mean you want to spend all your time with her.

6. If you care about your friendships, you owe it to your friends and yourself to at least talk about feeling excluded and find out what's going on.

Are You a Happy Camper?

Find out if you're too **careful** or too **carefree**.
Circle the letter next to the answer that describes you best.

1. It's the night before you leave for camp. As you lie in bed, you . . .

a. wonder whether you packed enough socks, who you'll sit with on the bus ride, if you'll get a top bunk, if the counselor will be nice, and who'll be in your cabin this year.

b. feel glad that you've already found a friend to sit with on the bus. But what if you get to the bus late and there are no empty seats left for you two to sit together?

c. get very excited about seeing all your old friends from last summer.

2. As you get ready to take your swimming test in the lake, you . . .

a. get a stomach ache. You're sure your legs will get tangled in that green stuff floating in the water.

b. get a little nervous about the water being too cold. You keep a sweatshirt nearby in case you get the shivers after your swim.

c. hope that this isn't going to take long so you can go back to the cabin and write your first letter home.

3. Your swim test lands you in the advanced class! The first thing you do is . . .

a. think it was a mistake and talk to a camp counselor about being put in the less advanced class where you'll feel safer.

b. see who else got into that class. Then find out if they're as nervous as you about learning lifesaving.

c. sign up to learn to water-ski on one ski— since you're finally qualified to try that.

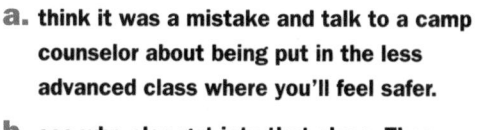

4. You wake up with a bug bite that itches a lot. Your friends tell you it's a mosquito bite. You . . .

a. are not so sure. After all, you've been eyeing a big spider up in the corner of your cabin. Keep checking it. By lunchtime decide to go see the nurse.

b. slather on the calamine lotion and promise yourself you'll go to the nurse if it's not better by tomorrow.

c. put on some anti-itch cream and head out for fun without giving it a second thought.

5. You've all gathered at the flagpole for a daylong hike. You're the one . . .

a. wearing white gook on your nose, a hat, bug repellent, sunscreen, and a backpack weighed down with a first aid kit and a rain poncho.

b. who remembered to wear and pack sunscreen, fill a canteen, and bring a snack. Still, you feel that you may be missing something, so you check your backpack one more time.

c. without sunscreen or even a hat. You figure you'll be fine. Besides, if you start to burn, you can always borrow someone else's sunscreen.

6. Tonight your group is camping out. You've just heard a ghost story and climbed into your sleeping bag. Now as the firelight casts shadows across your tent, the wind whistles through the trees, and an owl hoots, you . . .

a. are convinced that a ghost or monster is going to get you.

b. worry about bears but then remind yourself that the fire should keep them away—as long as the counselors stay up long enough to keep it lit. Hmmm . . .

c. feel kind of thrilled about being frightened and think about how it's moments like these that make camp so great.

7. Your friends want to raid the boys' camp. You're sure that if you do it, you'll . . .

a. get chased by the boys and sprain your ankle trying to run away. You try to talk your friends out of it.

b. get into trouble unless you do it right. You come up with a plan to pull off the raid without getting caught.

c. have tons of fun. You can't wait to get going. Is it dark enough yet?

8. On the last night of camp, everyone puts on a show. You and the girls in your cabin have worked out a skit. Now you're . . .

a. wishing you weren't in it. You're sure you'll forget your lines or trip onstage.

b. a little nervous, so you ask a friend to help you rehearse your lines.

c. wishing someone had a video camera to record your stellar performance.

SHOW TODAY

Answers

Mostly a's

Camp Oh-My-Gosh

The good news is you have a really active imagination. The bad news is that you tend to use it to spot potential dangers. It's important to think and plan ahead, but it's not good to fill yourself with dread. If you want to be a happier camper, think about the great things that could happen too!

Mostly b's

Camp Okee-Dokee

You worry a little but know when to stop. In fact, you know that there is a difference between getting yourself prepared and making yourself scared. So you try not to let your fears run away with you. Instead, you prepare just enough and then spend the rest of the time having fun.

Mostly c's

Camp What-Me-Worry?

You don't worry about events or stop to consider what could go wrong. You just enjoy doing things as they come along. This may work out well for you most of the time. But if you want to be a truly happy camper, think ahead a little more so you'll be prepared if trouble arises.

How Do You Doodle?

Are you a **shy sketcher** or a **daring designer?**
Find out what your doodles say about you!

Draw a **girl** in this box.

Draw a **tree** in this box.

Now circle the letter beside the answer that best describes your **girl doodle.**

1. My girl has eyes.

    a. no   **b.** yes

2. My girl has a mouth.

    a. no   **b.** yes

3. My girl has hands.

    a. no   **b.** yes

4. My girl has feet.

    a. no   **b.** yes

5. The lines in my drawing most closely match . . .

    a. this light stroke.   **b.** this medium stroke.   **c.** this heavy stroke.

6. My girl takes up . . .

    a. less than half the box.   **b.** exactly half the box.   **c.** more than half the box.

Scoring

Give yourself **1 point** for every **a** answer, **2 points** for every **b** answer, and **3 points** for every **c** answer. Then add them up to get your **girl score.**

1. _____

2. +_____

3. +_____

4. +_____

5. +_____

6. +_____

=_____ **girl score**

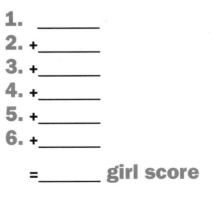

Now circle the letter beside the answer that best describes your **tree doodle.**

1. My tree has leaves.

    a. no   **b.** yes

2. My tree has branches.

    a. no   **b.** yes

3. My tree has a trunk that's an inch or wider.

    a. no   **b.** yes

4. My tree has grass growing around it.

    a. no   **b.** yes

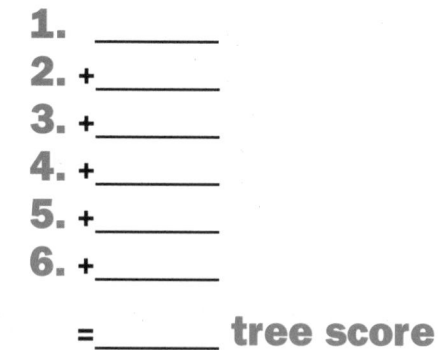

5. The lines in my drawing most closely match . . .

    a. this light stroke.   **b.** this medium stroke.   **c.** this heavy stroke.

6. My tree takes up . . .

    a. less than half the box.   **b.** exactly half the box.   **c.** more than half the box.

Scoring

Give yourself **1 point** for every **a** answer, **2 points** for every **b** answer, and **3 points** for every **c** answer. Then add them up to get your **tree score.**

1. _____

2. +_____

3. +_____

4. +_____

5. +_____

6. +_____

=_____ **tree score**

Now add your **girl score** and **tree score** together, then find out how you doodle.

_____ girl score

+_____ tree score

=_____ total doodle score

Answers

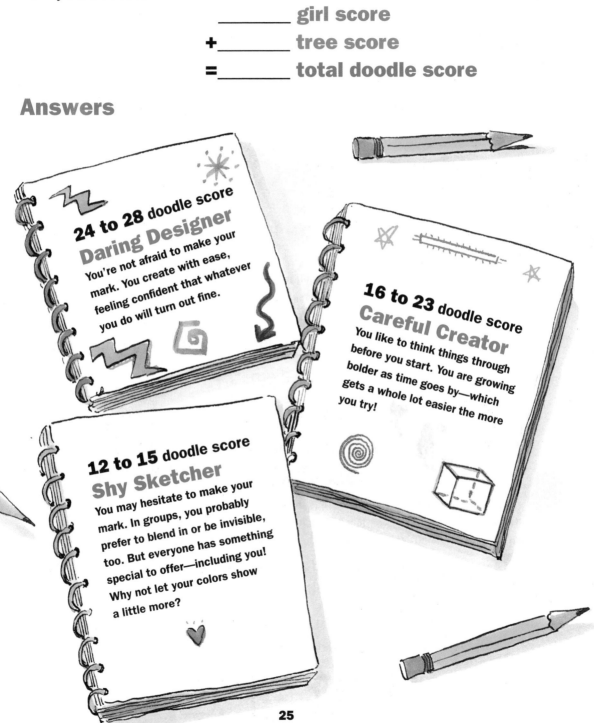

24 to 28 doodle score
Daring Designer
You're not afraid to make your mark. You create with ease, feeling confident that whatever you do will turn out fine.

16 to 23 doodle score
Careful Creator
You like to think things through before you start. You are growing bolder as time goes by—which gets a whole lot easier the more you try!

12 to 15 doodle score
Shy Sketcher
You may hesitate to make your mark. In groups, you probably prefer to blend in or be invisible, too. But everyone has something special to offer—including you! Why not let your colors show a little more?

Tidy Test

Are you **pretty neat** or **mostly messy?** Circle
the letter next to the answer that describes you best.

1. When you get dressed for school in the morning, you . . .

a. put on the outfit you laid out last night.

b. look around in the closet for a while until you find your favorite shirt.

c. rummage through the laundry basket for something clean to wear.

2. When you want to put your hair up in a ponytail, you can find your favorite scrunchie . . .

a. stretched around the handle of your hairbrush where you always keep it.

b. on your dresser with all your other hair thingies.

c. under your bed with dust bunnies the size of Ping-Pong balls.

3. At the bottom of your backpack, you're most likely to find . . .

a. a pencil case.

b. an extra pair of gloves, pens, and a note from a friend.

c. empty candy wrappers, old tissues, and the lunch money you thought you lost the other day.

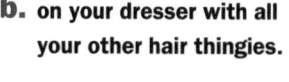 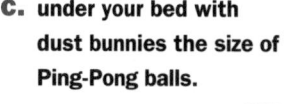

4. Your school locker is . . .

a. neat as a pin.   **b.** a little cluttered.   **c.** a disaster area.

5. During English class, you hand in a book report. Your paper looks . . .

a. perfect.   **b.** a little smudged but readable.   **c.** like your dog really did eat it.

6. You get caught in a thunderstorm on your way home from school. When you walk in the door cold and wet, you . . .

a. take off your boots and put them on a mat by the door to dry.

b. kick off your boots as you run to the bathroom to get some tissues.

c. head to the kitchen to make hot chocolate, leaving a trail of puddles along the way.

7. You eat a bowl of ice cream while doing homework in your room. When you're finished, you . . .

a. wash and dry the bowl and spoon, then put them away.

b. rinse the bowl and spoon, then leave them in the kitchen sink.

c. set the bowl and spoon on your nightstand. You'll take them to the kitchen in the morning.

8. When it's time to hit the sack, your bed is . . .

a. neatly made.

b. tousled but tidy.

c. hidden by clothes and magazines.

Answers

Mostly a's
Pretty Neat
You tidy up and organize wherever you go. Keeping things clean and orderly helps you focus on more important stuff throughout the day.

Mostly b's
Kinda Comfy
You're comfortable with a little clutter. Your room just wouldn't feel like a place you could relax or play if *everything* were organized and tucked away. Besides, you can probably find the important things when you need them.

Mostly c's
Mostly Messy
No doubt about it—you're messy. Wouldn't it be nice to find things when you need them? You may want to try setting aside a little time each week to put your things in order.

Are You Too Nice?

Are you a **marshmallow softie** or a **smart cookie?**
Circle the letter next to the answer that describes you best.

1. You've been waiting in line at the snack counter forever. When it's finally your turn, another girl butts in line ahead of you. You . . .

a. try to remember that who goes first really doesn't matter in the big picture of things and wait patiently to place your order next.

b. glare at her so that she knows just how disgusted you are with her piggy behavior.

c. say, "Excuse me, but I believe it was my turn next." Then place your order.

2. Your social studies group has been assigned a project for class, but you're the only one doing any work. You . . .

a. do all the work. You don't want to let the group down.

b. grumble a lot while doing the work and hope the others get the hint.

c. explain that it's not fair to have you do all the work and ask the others to pitch in.

3. You bundle up for the walk to school, but the girl you walk with doesn't because she thinks it's uncool. Now she's asking to borrow your hat for the third time this week. You . . .

a. hand it over. How can you let her shiver?

b. tell her no at first but then give in when she starts to cough and sniffle.

c. say you'd rather not because you hate it when your head gets cold.

4. "You look adorable. Let's buy it!" squeals Mom while adjusting the collar on the polka-dot dress you're trying on. You . . .

   a. say "O.K." and promise yourself that you'll only wear the dress to Grandma's house. That way none of your friends will see you in it.

   b. shrug your shoulders and let Mom buy it. You'll hang it in your closet and hope she forgets about it.

   c. say, "I'll never wear it. Can we find something else that we both like?"

5. A friend keeps blowing off your plans at the last minute. You . . .

   a. understand and forgive her. She always has a good reason.

   b. know you should tell her how disappointed you are, but you don't. You don't want her to get mad.

   c. tell her how you feel and how you want to be treated. Then give her a chance to change her ways.

6. You're at the mall with your best friend when you both spot a fabulous T-shirt at the same time. You . . .

   a. let her buy it. That's what a good friend does, right?

   b. tell your friend you don't think it's a good color for her and hope that she'll lose interest so you can buy it.

   c. suggest that you each buy one in a different color.

7. You're sure you ordered fries with your cheeseburger, but you get a baked potato instead. You . . .

   a. say nothing. A baked potato is healthier anyway.

   b. ask your dad if he'll swap his fries for your potato.

   c. tell the waitress that there's been a mistake.

8. You invite two friends over to play a new board game, but while you're reading the instructions they decide they'd rather go Rollerblading. You . . .

a. go along with them despite feeling disappointed. You don't want to force them to do something they don't want to do.

b. come up with reasons why their plan won't work: there's too much traffic, your skating socks aren't clean, and it looks like it's going to rain.

c. tell them how disappointed you feel and talk them into giving the game a chance.

Answers

Mostly a's
Marshmallow Softie

You may be too soft and sweet for your own good. You get stuck doing things you don't like to do and give up what you want just to please others or to keep the peace. Next time you start to soften, ask yourself what it is that *you* really want or think. Then speak up and see what happens. You'll feel stronger having done so.

Mostly b's
Candy-Coated Peanut

You may be sweet on the outside but going nuts underneath. You know what you want and how you really feel about things. The problem is you don't say it. Don't expect people to read your mind— speak up! Saying what you want may be hard at first, but it will get easier with practice.

Mostly c's
Chocolate-Chip Cookie

You're a smart cookie who is chock-full of sweetness! You understand that it's important to speak up for yourself in a semisweet way and let the chips fall where they may. People are likely to respect your honesty and confidence.

Good Cents

Imagine you just received **$50** for your birthday.
How would you **spend** it? Answer the questions
and **keep track** of what you make or spend.

1. At the bookstore, you find two new titles from your favorite mystery
series. You . . .

a. buy one now and wait until you finish it before buying the other.

$3.50

b. buy both of them. Who knows if you'll find these titles again?

$7.00

c. wait and borrow them from the library.

$0

$ _7.00_

2. For lunch at the pool, you . . .

a. get a cheeseburger, fries, and a soda at the snack shop.

$3.00

b. eat the lunch you packed.

$0

c. order in a pizza with the works for you and your friends.

$10.00

$ _3.00_

3. Hot dogs are two for $1.00 at the ballpark today. You . . .

a. buy two, even though just one will fill you up.

$1.00

b. buy a bag of chips to hold you over till dinner.

25¢

c. buy one.

50¢

$ _50¢_

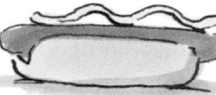

4. At the school carnival, you spot a cute stuffed gorilla prize. You . . .

a. throw darts until the gorilla is yours!

b. pass it by, knowing you could buy one for less than it would take to win it.

c. throw a few darts but give up after three tries.

$10.00

$0

$3.00

$ _O_

5. Your neighbor is having a garage sale. You . . .

a. buy a faded pair of jeans to cut into shorts for summer.

b. buy a ton of stuff, even if you don't really need it. Everything's so cheap!

c. set up a lemonade stand for thirsty sale-goers.

$2.00

$5.00

Make $8.00!

$ _2.00_

6. When you hear the ice cream truck coming down the street, you . . .

a. run outside and buy a supersize rocket pop with bubble gum inside.

b. wander over and buy a Popsicle to split with your brother.

c. go to the freezer and pop out the orange juice cubes you froze earlier.

$1.00

50¢

$0

$ _50¢_

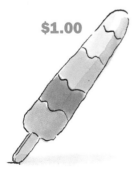

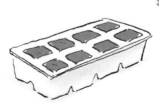

7. A friend invited you to her birthday slumber party. You go shopping for a gift and buy . . .

a. a poster of Rocky Rockburn, everyone's favorite rock star— last year. It's on sale.

$2.00

b. a scrapbook for the birthday girl to put all her party photos in.

$8.00

c. earrings for your friend and PJ's for yourself. You want to have the best PJ's at the party.

$15.00 $ _8.00_

Answers

Subtract or add what you spent or made from **$50.**

$50.00 **Birthday Money**
− $2̶1.00 **Money Spent**
+ 0 **Money Earned**
= 21.00 **Total Left**

$10 or Less Left
Hole in Your Pocket?

Money probably slips easily through your fingers. Before your funds dry up, think before you buy. Do you really need that stuffed gorilla? Try saving some money or even making a little of your own.

$11 to $34 Left
Money Minder

You're a smart spender and a savvy saver. You like to treat yourself every now and then, but you also know not to give in to spur-of-the-moment spending.

$35 or More Left
Smart Saver

You'd rather save money than spend it. Even when you do spend money, you're usually very resourceful about it. Your good cents may add up to a fortune-filled future!

Silly Scale

Are you **hungry** for **humor?** Weigh in on the silly scale to find out. Circle the letter next to the answer that fits you best.

1. People are more likely to tell you . . .

a. "Lighten up!"

b. "Stop fooling around!"

2. When you're with a group of classmates or friends, you tend to . . .

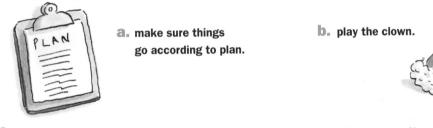

a. make sure things go according to plan.

b. play the clown.

3. When your parents describe you to other adults, they usually say . . .

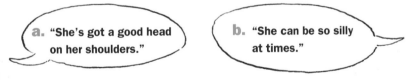

a. "She's got a good head on her shoulders."

b. "She can be so silly at times."

4. If you could choose where to go on your next class field trip, you would choose . . .

a. the planetarium.

b. the jelly bean factory.

5. When someone makes a joke in class, you usually . . .

    a. giggle and then get back to what you were doing.

    b. laugh and shout out a joke of your own.

6. To you a great gift would be . . .

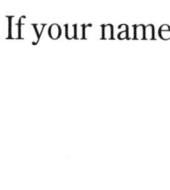

    a. a book about cats.

    b. a book of knock-knock jokes.

7. If your name was Nicole, you'd prefer to be called . . .

    a. Nicole

    b.

8. The first part of the Sunday newspaper you read is . . .

    a. the front page.

    b. the comics.

9. When you get to pick what to watch on TV, you choose . . .

    a. soap operas.

    b. cartoons.

Answers

0 to 3 b's = Silly   **4 or 5 b's = Sillier**   **6 to 9 b's = silliest**

You tend to view giggling and goofing around like cookies and ice cream: as rewards they're great, but first you want to clean your plate. You prefer to get work done before you have fun.

When you have to decide between work and play, your appetite for amusement sometimes points the way. So if a friend starts joking around, you'll join in on the fun.

You might say that giggles are your favorite snacks since you love to laugh. You're often the one cooking up the fun for yourself and friends.

Do You Dare?

Are you **bold** and **brave** or do you **look** before you **leap?**
Circle the letter next to the answer that describes you best.

1. You've never had sushi before. So when you
go out to eat at a Japanese restaurant for
Mom's birthday, you . . .

a. order the shrimp since you know what that's like.

b. go for the raw eel sashimi with fish eggs on top.
You can't knock it until you try it, right?

c. ask the waiter, "Are you sure you don't have
any hamburgers?"

2. You've always dreamed about being onstage.
When you see a poster for a school musical,
you decide to . . .

a. audition for the chorus. If you mess up,
the others will cover for you.

b. try out for the lead part. Someone has
to get it. It might as well be you!

c. volunteer for the stage crew. Although you'd
love to be the star, it's just too scary.

3. You're having dinner at your aunt's house with
three exchange students from Argentina.
Everyone is speaking Spanish. You . . .

a. smile a lot but keep quiet and motion
for the butter when you need it.

b. say all the Spanish words you know
and learn new ones, too!

c. hang out with your uncle in the kitchen,
where things aren't so confusing.

4. You go boating with a friend and her family. After you watch everyone else water-ski, they ask if you'd like to try. You . . .

  a. ask a lot of questions first.

  b. dive right in.

  c. change the subject by asking, "When's lunch?"

5. You make a pact with a friend to paint your faces for the big Bobcats game. You . . .

  a. paint two small stripes on your cheek. You don't want to look too goofy.

  b. paint a stripe down your nose, "Go Cats" on one cheek, and a paw print on the other.

  c. chicken out and avoid your friend at the game.

6. You're at the airport picking up Grandma when you spy your favorite rock star on the moving walkway. You . . .

  a. follow her until she disappears into a "members only" lounge.

  b. rush up to her and start chatting. Then ask for an autograph.

  c. try not to stare.

Answers

Mostly a's
Look, Then Leap
You dare with care. You like to ask questions and think about the risks before taking the plunge and having fun.

Mostly b's
Bold and Brave
You don't think twice about doing new and different things. You figure you won't know if you like it until you try it.

Mostly c's
Safe, Not Sorry
You go with what you know and do what feels comfortable. Just remember that doing or learning something new can be fun, too!

Pal Poll

Answer these questions with a **friend** in mind,
then ask her to check your answers.

1. The three things my friend likes best about herself are

_____ ,

_____ ,

and _____ .

2. Her most prized possession is her _____ .

3. The best birthday present she could get is

_____ .

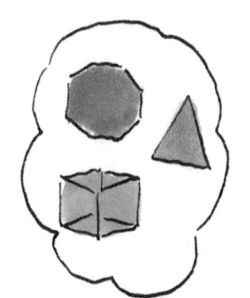

4. Her pet peeve is _____

_____ .

5. She would most likely doodle . . .

a. cute puppies, kitties, or stick people.

b. flowers, trees, a sun, or a moon.

c. stars, arrows, hearts, or curlicues.

d. triangles, boxes, or other geometric shapes.

6. She would be least likely to do the following in front of other people . . .

a. sing a solo. **b.** dance. **c.** give an oral report. **d.** act in a play.

7. Her favorite flavor of ice cream is _____.

8. Her favorite color of jelly bean is _____.

9. When it comes to snacking, she has . . .

a. a sweet tooth. **b.** salt attacks. **c.** healthy habits. **d.** a spicy streak.

10. Her favorite music group or singer is _____.

11. The movie that she would rent again and again is

_____.

12. The movie that she would never rent or go to see is

_____.

13. The one TV show she never misses is _____

_____.

14. She always says _____.

15. Her favorite place to be alone is _____.

16. She usually does her homework . . .

a. in front of the TV. **b.** in her room. **c.** at the kitchen table. **d.** with me!

17. Her favorite amusement park ride is _____.

18. Her favorite holiday is _____.

19. Her dream vacation is _____

_____.

20. She would say that it's more important to be . . .

a. smart.   **b.** pretty.   **c.** wealthy.   **d.** athletic.

Answers

Score **1 point** for each correct answer.

16 to 20 points

You must care a lot about your friend to know her as well as you do—inside out and through and through. If she knows you as well as you know her, you're a lucky pair!

10 to 15 points

You know your friend very well, but you still discover something new every now and then. That's all part of the fun of becoming even better friends.

0 to 9 points

There's always more to learn about a friend. You two probably have a lot of discoveries ahead of you. Explore and enjoy!

Pssst!

Can you **keep** a **secret?** Circle the answer that
most closely describes what you'd do in each situation.

1. Your friend Chelsea told you what song she's
singing at her audition for the musical and
made you promise not to tell anyone. You . . .

   a. keep it to yourself.

   b. tell only your best friend—she's not trying out
for the musical anyway.

   c. tell everyone who's auditioning so they'll
know how close you and Chelsea are.

2. You and your friends have planned a surprise
pizza party for Tracey tonight. So when
Tracey orders pizza for lunch, you . . .

   a. say nothing and hope she likes pizza
a whole lot!

   b. say, "But that's what . . . you had yesterday,"
catching yourself midsentence.

   c. blurt out, "But we're having pizza tonight. Oops!"

3. When no one is looking, Grandma slips you $10.
"Here's a little reward for your good grades. It'll
be our secret," she whispers. You . . .

   a. smile and quickly stuff the money in your pocket.

   b. are so excited, you have to tell Dad immediately.
Too bad your brother overhears you.

   c. wave the $10 bill in your brother's face
as soon as you leave Grandma's house.

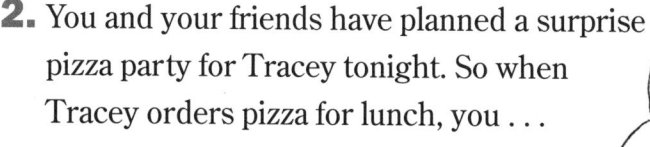

4. You overhear your math teacher say he's getting engaged over break. When you congratulate him later, he asks you to keep it a secret so the class doesn't get distracted. You . . .

a. do—even though you're dying to tell the whole school.

b. tell a few friends but don't name any names.

c. squeal, squeal, squeal! News this big is too exciting not to reveal!

5. You see your friend Melissa at the store buying a training bra. Melissa gets really embarrassed and asks you not to tell anyone. You . . .

a. keep her secret. You wouldn't want anyone blabbing the news when your day comes.

b. tell only your best friend. She just got a bra, too, and will understand.

c. talk about how many girls in class have bras at recess the next day. You include Melissa in the list.

6. You see your brother out riding his bike—but he's supposed to be grounded! He begs you to keep quiet about it. You . . .

a. pretend you never saw him.

b. wave and give him a big, cheesy smile. Now he *has* to let you use the computer whenever you want—or else!

c. rush home and tell Mom. It's payback time.

Answers

Mostly a's
Lips Are Sealed

Secrets are safe with you! Once your lips are sealed, you throw away the key. Bravo! You have a good understanding of privacy and know the value of keeping your word. You probably don't even reveal the things you've accidentally seen or overheard.

Mostly b's
Sometimes Slip

You know when you shouldn't be letting a secret out, but sometimes it just slips. And other times you can't resist the excitement of being the one to share great gossip. But you know that you can do better at keeping your lips sealed. Listen to your conscience and think before you speak. Others will be glad you did!

Mostly c's
Loose Lips

Your loose lips let everything slip. When you break your word about keeping a secret, you show people that they can't count on you to be trustworthy. Unless you're willing to let your friendships suffer and get a reputation as a big blabbermouth, it's time to take your promises more seriously and keep those secrets to yourself. Zip those lips!

Are You a Class Act?

What's your **school style?** Circle the letter next to
the answer that describes you best.

1. When the class bell rings, you're . . .

a. at your desk with your
pencil sharpened and
notebook open.

b. rooting around in your
desk for your lucky
purple pencil.

c. hanging out at the
pencil sharpener,
waving to the cars
that drive by outside.

2. When you glance at your weekly planner, you find . . .

a. test dates and
assignments listed.

b. dozens of doodles.

c. Who needs a planner
when you can call your
friends?

3. Before the weekly vocabulary test, you . . .

a. quiz yourself with flash
cards each night.

b. read the definitions
over and over again
while eating breakfast
the morning of the test.

c. ask to go see the
school nurse as soon
as your teacher starts
handing out the test.

4. While studying fossils in science class, you . . .

a. take notes about all
the neat rocks.

b. use the magnifying
glass to examine your
hair cuticles.

c. daydream about
dinosaurs.

5. Class elections are coming up. You . . .

a. run for president!

b. vote for the girl who is having a slumber party next weekend.

c. draw mustaches on the campaign posters hanging in the hall.

6. Your English teacher drops a hint that there might be a pop quiz on Friday. You . . .

a. make a note in your planner.

b. make a mental note to remember to study.

c. sigh and roll your eyes.

7. You're in social studies class, dying to talk with your best friend. You . . .

a. plan to catch her right after class.

b. try to listen to what the teacher is saying as you dash off a short note to her.

c. tune out the teacher and write your friend a two-page note, pass it along, and watch her read it.

8. When your teacher asks a question in class, you usually . . .

a. raise your hand to answer.

b. wait to be called upon, even though you think you know the answer.

c. hide behind your book.

9. When your class goes to the library, you . . .

a. find a book for your next report.

b. whisper, giggle, and get "shushed" by the librarian.

c. curl up on the reading chair with a Gameboy.

10. A friend invites you to her house after school, but a book report is due tomorrow. You . . .

a. tell your friend you'll come another day.

b. go for a little while and plan to stay up late to finish the book.

c. go and have a great time, then ask your sister to tell you what the book is about.

Answers

Mostly **a**'s

Class Act

You're putting all you've got into your schoolwork. And you're a lucky girl because you know that the more you put into what you do, the more you get out of it.

Mostly **b**'s

Class Passer

Sometimes you try, but other times you do just enough to get by. You're probably giving school only half your effort— and you're probably only getting half back.

Mostly **c**'s

Class Slacker

Your body may be present at school, but your mind is most likely to be absent. If you pay more attention and put your heart into your work, you may find that it feels good to be part of the class.

Moment of Truth

How **honest** are you? Circle the letter next to the answer
that most closely describes what you'd do in each situation.

1. You knew all the words for the Spanish test—or at least you thought you did.
But now that you're taking the test, there's one word you can't recall. You . . .

a. whisper to the girl next to you and ask
for the answer.

b. try to spot the word on another girl's test.

c. guess as well as you can and hope you can
make up for any wrong answers with extra
credit points.

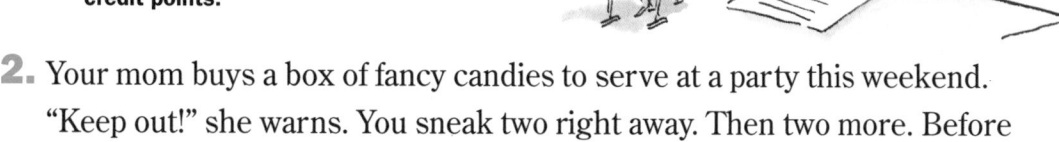

2. Your mom buys a box of fancy candies to serve at a party this weekend.
"Keep out!" she warns. You sneak two right away. Then two more. Before
you know it, you've eaten half the box. You . . .

a. wait to see what happens. Your little
brother usually gets blamed for these sorts
of things.

b. decide to secretly replace the box and hope
your mom won't notice.

c. tell your mom and offer to pay for a new box
out of your allowance.

3. You're playing cards with a friend at the beach when you realize you can
see all her cards reflected in her sunglasses. You . . .

a. win the game. Hooray!

b. try not to look but peek when you're
not sure which card to play.

c. tell her about it and deal a new hand—
one she plays with her sunglasses off.

4. At lunch your friends ask about the poem you wrote for English class. "What poem?" you ask, suddenly remembering one was due today. You . . .

- **a.** rush to the library, copy a poem out of a book, and put your name on it.

- **b.** pretend to have a stomach ache and go to the school nurse to buy yourself time.

- **c.** try to write something in a hurry. If you can't, explain to your teacher that you messed up and ask for an extension.

5. You accidentally hit a neighbor's window with a Frisbee. Your neighbor storms across the street and demands an apology just as your dad pulls up in the driveway and automatically jumps to your defense. You . . .

- **a.** deny it. What's the big deal? You didn't break it.

- **b.** say nothing but feel terrible and worry about what your dad would think if he knew the truth.

- **c.** share the truth with Dad and apologize to your neighbor.

6. You're helping out at a local orchard and getting paid for each apple you pick. Your sister asks you if she can help out for fun. You . . .

- **a.** let her help but don't tell her about the money you're making from her apples. She'll never know.

- **b.** let her help, then use some of your earnings to treat her to ice cream.

- **c.** tell her you're getting paid for the apples. Then you give her what she earns to put in her piggy bank.

7. When the movie is over at the multiplex cinema, you and your friend suddenly realize how easy it would be to sneak into another movie. You . . .

a. think it's a great idea and follow your friend to the next theater.

b. do it but worry the whole time about getting caught.

c. regret missing the movie but don't sneak in because it's wrong.

8. You loan your sister a jacket. When you get it back, you find $10 in the pocket. You . . .

a. consider it payment for the loan and go shopping!

b. convince yourself it might have been yours. It was in a small pocket she might not have used or even noticed.

c. ask your sister if it's hers.

Answers

If you answered a more than once . . .
Pants on Fire?

Be careful. One lie or dishonest act often leads to another. What's more, lies often hurt others and may ultimately hurt you. So what should you do? Tell the truth!

Mostly b's
Stretching the Truth

You tend to let the truth go unsaid when hiding it will benefit you. The thing is, you know you're being dishonest, and that doesn't feel too good inside. You'll feel better once you start being completely honest with yourself and others.

Mostly c's
Nothing but the Truth

You know what's right, and you usually do it. Even when you mess up, you're willing to fess up and take responsibility for your actions. Bravo! Stay true to yourself and keep your conscience free.

Friendship Rings

Get together with a **friend** and discover your **likes** and **dislikes**.

1. On a piece of paper, **write** down your **top ten things** in one of the categories at the right. Have your friend do the same, but don't talk about them until you're finished.

2. Compare your lists and **circle** any items you both listed. Then **write** these items in the **middle** of one of the sets of rings on the following pages.

3. Write the other items on your list to the side in one ring, and have your friend **list** the rest of her items in the other ring.

Friendship Ring Categories
▪ Cartoon Characters
▪ Wild Animals
▪ Snacks
▪ Sounds
▪ Board Games
▪ Books
▪ Road Trips
▪ TV Shows
▪ Pet Peeves
▪ Amusement Park Rides
▪ Sports to Play

Top Ten Dream Vacations

Mine
- Amsterdam
- San Francisco
- Grand Canyon
- Alaska
- Ocean City

Ours
- Sea World
- London
- Australia
- Hawaii
- Olympics

Yours
- Williamsburg
- Outer Banks
- Italy
- Chicago
- Spain

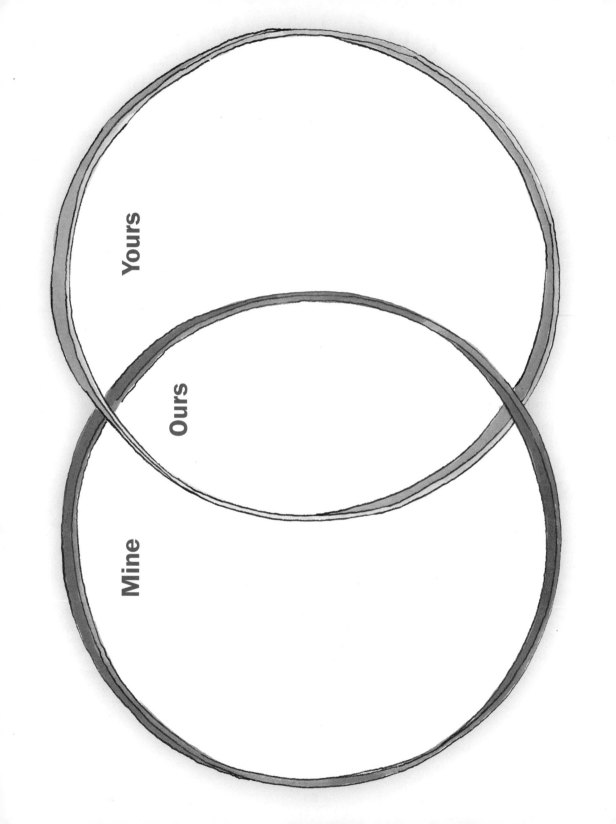

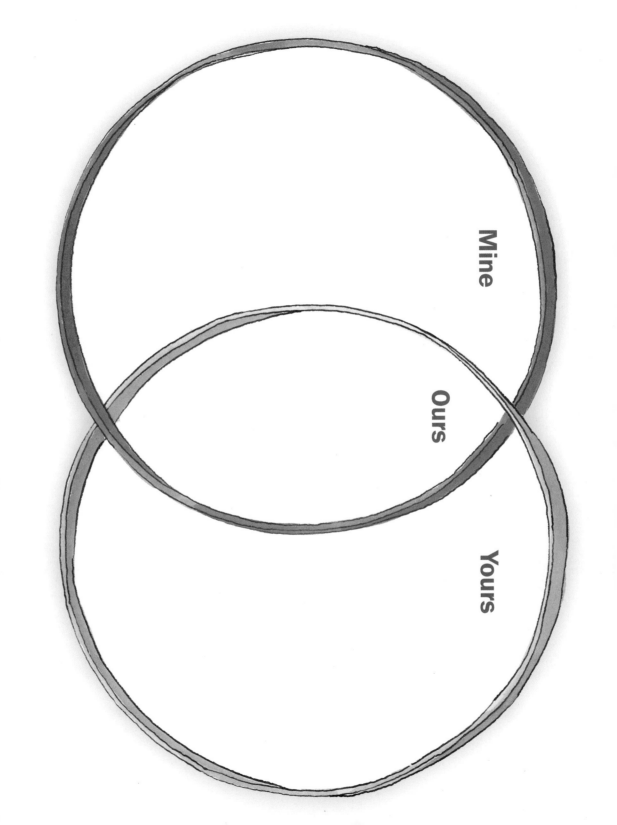

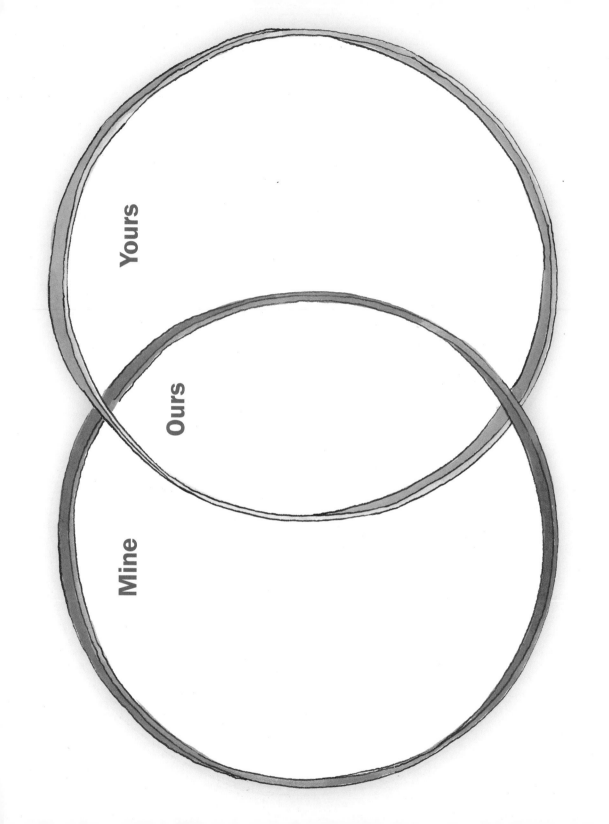

Reading Your Rings

One circle represents you, and the other represents your friend. The place where they **overlap** is where your likes or interests **blend.** The more things you have in the **middle** of the circles, the more **alike** you and your friend are. See how many favorites you **share.** Then pick another category and fill in more rings. If you run out of rings or categories, make up your own!

If you share . . .

5 or More Favorites
You're two peas in a pod. You have a lot in common and like to do many of the same things.

3 to 4 Favorites
You share many likes, but you also do different things from time to time.

1 to 2 Favorites
Did you learn something new about your likes and dislikes? Just because you don't have much in common in this area doesn't mean you don't have grounds for a great friendship. Choose another category and keep searching for what you both like.

What If Your Likes Just Never Overlap?
Opposites also attract! You two have fun sharing and exploring your likes and interests.

Losing Your Cool

What do you do when you **lose** your **cool?**
Circle the letter next to the answer that most closely describes what you'd do in each situation.

1. When you ask your friend Zoe to go swimming, she says she doesn't want to go to the pool today. So you go alone. But when you get there, you see Zoe hanging out—with another girl! You . . .

a. say, "Hey! Some friend you are!"

b. make a quick exit so no one will see you cry.

c. leave before they spot you, and never mention the incident.

d. forget Zoe and look for other friends.

2. During a big soccer game, you pass the ball to Nina. But the other team steals it from her and makes the winning goal. You . . .

a. yell at Nina, "You blew it!"

b. feel like crying.

c. act like this is no big deal, even though you're a little disappointed.

d. tell your teammates never to pass the ball to Nina again.

3. You're working on a project with your friend Amy. You write a good report, but Amy makes a sloppy poster to go along with it. Your team gets a low grade. You . . .

   a. say, "I can't believe what a sloppy person you are! I'm never going to team up with you again."

   b. get so upset you start to cry.

   c. don't say anything because you don't want Amy to feel bad.

   d. make sure everyone knows the low grade was Amy's fault.

4. Your dad promised to take you to the school carnival. But by the time he gets home, it's too late to go. You . . .

   a. shout, "Thanks for nothing!" then stomp off and slam the door to your room.

   b. watch TV as tears fill your eyes.

   c. tell him it's O.K.—even though it's not.

   d. give him the silent treatment for the whole week.

5. Your sister borrows your best shirt and returns it covered with stains. You . . .

   a. yell, "What a pig! I'm never loaning you anything of mine again!"

   b. try to wash out the stains as tears stream down your cheeks.

   c. say nothing. Your parents will be furious if you start arguing.

   d. take back the bracelet you gave her for her birthday.

6. You've made plans to go to the park with friends, but Mom says you have to stay home and help clean the house. You . . .

a. scowl and shout, "I never get to have any fun!"

b. sniffle and sulk while folding the laundry.

c. take a deep breath and go get the furniture polish.

d. put darks and whites together in the same wash. Next time Mom won't want your help.

Answers

Mostly a's

You tend to blurt hurtful words or act in loud, stormy ways when you're angry. Whether you do these things on purpose to get your point across or because you can't help it, consider this: yelling mean things or slamming doors doesn't really tell others why you're angry. So, you'd be better off saying, "I'm so mad I need time to cool down!" Then take a few deep breaths, count to ten, or even go away for a while. You can come back and talk when you've recovered from being so mad.

Mostly b's

Crying is probably your way of getting your strong feelings out. In fact, it may be hard for you to put your angry feelings into words. It's O.K. to cry, but once you have, you may want to wash your face and then try to talk calmly about what made you so angry.

Mostly c's

You often cover up angry feelings because you don't want to hurt anyone or you figure that sharing how you feel won't make a difference anyway.

Actually, though, hiding your feelings can hurt you and your relationships, and it won't make things better. Tell people how you feel so that whatever bothered you in the first place is less likely to happen again.

Mostly d's

You have a tendency to want to "get even" with whoever has made you angry or to "make them see how they made you feel." Getting even or inflicting a similar hurt may seem fair, but it usually just makes things worse. If you really want to make things better, talk them over with the person you're angry with.

Can You Read Minds?

Body language can sometimes give you clues about what others are **thinking** or **feeling.**

Write the **letter** of each classmate next to what he or she **appears** to be **thinking.**

⭐ __C__ **1.** "Is it my turn yet? I'm so nervous."

⭐ __f__ **2.** "Whatever."

⭐ __d__ **3.** "Wow! That's cool."

⭐ __b__ **4.** "I'm grumpy. When's lunch?"

⭐ __a__ **5.** "I can't wait to go to the slumber party tonight."

⭐ __e__ **6.** "Huh? I don't get it."

Answers
1. c; 2. f; 3. d; 4. b; 5. a; 6. e

The Write Clues

Does your handwriting hold clues about you? Write and see.

Write a paragraph in the box below about anything at all. Don't try to make your handwriting come out a certain way. Just think about what you want to say so that you write naturally.

Now circle the letter next to the answer that best describes your handwriting.

1. How do your letters slant?

a. to the left
slant

b. to the right
slant

c. not much at all
slant

What it might mean:

a. You're quiet, calm, and focused.

b. You plunge ahead with courage, enthusiasm, and a sense of adventure.

c. You're practical and reliable. You're often the one who gets the job done.

2. How hard do you press when you write?

a. not very hard

b. hard *girl*

c. medium *girl*

What it might mean:

a. You're gentle, sensitive, and a little shy. Sometimes you want to hide like invisible ink.

b. You're energetic, forceful, and bold—unafraid to make your mark or speak your mind.

c. You don't get pushy or get pushed around. Instead, you strike a happy medium between bossy and laid-back.

3. How wide are your letters? Draw a box around an "n" to find out.

a. Is the box a perfect square? *rainbow*

b. Is it wider than it is tall? *rainbow*

c. Is it taller than it is wide? *rainbow*

What it might mean:

a. You strike a balance between work and play.

b. You're friendly and chatty.

c. You like to focus on your goals before having a good time.

4. How do you cross your lowercase t's?

a. straight across

𝓉

b. slanting up

𝓉

c. slanting down

𝓉

What it might mean:

a. You're approaching tasks with confidence and care.

b. You're aiming high and feeling ambitious.

c. You're getting down to work and going after what you want—and with your determination and persistence, you may just get it, too.

5. Where do you dot your lowercase i's?

a. a little to the right of the i

𝓲

b. a little to the left of the i

𝓲

c. exactly above the i

𝓲

What it might mean:

a. You make decisions quickly. You like to work fast and not worry about the details.

b. You tend to put things off until later.

c. You crave perfection and try to be precise in all you do.

6. What do the lower loops on your letters look like?

a. long and full

loopy

b. big and round

loopy

c. long or hooked but not fully looped

loopy

d. so short and thin that they're not really there

loopy

What it might mean:

a. Whether you're running for class president or trying out for band soloist, you want to be the center of attention.

b. From playing sports to baking cookies, you like to keep busy.

c. When it comes to math equations, mystery novels, even jigsaw puzzles, you won't quit until you find a solution.

d. You're a practical-minded girl who likes to find the fastest way to do something. You take the shortcut home from school and pop popcorn in the microwave.

7. Now look at the lines you wrote. Do they go . . .

a. uphill

We went to the beach.

b. downhill

We went to the beach.

c. up and down like waves

We went to the beach.

What it might mean:

a. You're feeling happy.

b. You're feeling blue.

c. Your feelings may be just like the lines of your handwriting: up one minute and down the next.

Parent Poll

How well do you know **Mom** or **Dad?** Take this quiz with a
parent in mind, then ask him or her to check your answers.

1. Middle name _____

2. Age _____

3. Place of birth _____

4. Nickname _____

5. Color of eyes _____

6. Right- or left-handed _____

7. Best friend _____

8. Favorite relative _____

9. Official title at work

10. Dream job

11. Most admired person

12. Favorite author

13. Least favorite chore

14. Favorite recipe to make

15. Favorite restaurant

16. Favorite family vacation spot

17. Front, back, or middle of roller coaster

18. Favorite sport ....

19. Favorite day of the year ....

20. Favorite thing to do on Saturday afternoon ....

....

21. Least favorite word that you say

....

22. Pet peeve (the one thing that really drives him or her crazy)

....

23. Favorite room in the house ....

24. The one thing he or she can't leave home without

....

25. Favorite music ....

26. Favorite radio station ....

27. Favorite movie star

28. Word or phrase said most often

29. Worst present ever received

30. Favorite pizza topping

Answers
Score **1 point** for each question you answered correctly.

20 to 30 points
Parent Pal
You're in tight with Mom or Dad. Knowing your parent so well shows how much you care.

10 to 19 points
Family Familiar
You're pretty familiar with Mom or Dad—and now you know even more!

0 to 9 points
Parent Dare
Dare to know your parent better. Take time to notice likes and dislikes, habits or hobbies. There's lots more to share.

Are You Ready for a Pet?

Should you go for the **golden retriever** or
stick to **stuffed animals?** Take this quiz to find out.

1. It's your week to care for the class rabbit, and you notice you're running
low on food. You . . .

    a. write a note for the teacher to let her know.

    b. guess that you have enough left for a couple
more days. You can always feed the bunny
carrots if you run out.

    c. forget about it. The teacher will take care of it.

2. When you visit your friend, her puppy Poochie always barks and jumps
on you, even though your friend doesn't want him to. You . . .

    a. say, "Sit, Poochie!" in a loud, stern voice, just
as your friend learned at obedience school.

    b. try to hold Poochie back until he calms down.

    c. clap your hands and encourage Poochie to jump
and bark more. It's fun—even if he's misbehaving.

3. You're picking up your friend for a movie when she discovers that Poochie
has had another accident on the kitchen floor. "Oh, no!" she says and runs
for the paper towels. You . . .

    a. volunteer to take Poochie outside for a couple
of minutes while your friend cleans up the mess.

    b. wait impatiently while your friend scrambles to wipe
up the puddle and takes Poochie for a quick walk.

    c. tell her to leave the mess for her mom to clean
up. You're in a hurry.

4. When Aunt Susan brings her cat Raku over to stay with your family while she's on vacation, you . . .

a. say hi to Raku and scratch her under the chin—her favorite spot. Then get the lowdown from your aunt about how to care for Raku.

b. chase Raku around the room and pick her up, even though she seems a little scared. You love cuddling cats!

c. ask your aunt, "Do I really have to clean her litter box *every* day?"

5. When Raku wakes you up early the next morning by nuzzling your face and purring very loudly, you . . .

a. cuddle for a minute, then get up and feed her.

b. throw a sock on the floor for her to play with, then pull the covers up over your head and try to go back to sleep.

c. put her out in the hall. Maybe someone else will get up and feed her.

6. When you go downstairs to get your soccer jersey from the laundry, you notice that Raku's cat litter box smells bad. You . . .

a. change the litter and take the smelly stuff out to the trash can.

b. scoop out the lumps for now. You'll change the litter after the game . . . if you remember.

c. spray air freshener around the litter box, then skip off to the soccer game.

Answers

Mostly a's

With your sense of commitment and responsibility, you have the potential to become a great pet owner. There's a lot to consider when you get a new critter. So read up and learn even more about your new pet before bringing it home.

Mostly b's

You may not be prepared to take care of a pet that needs a lot of attention or to train an animal to behave properly. Before you get a pet of your own, try taking care of someone else's pet first. Volunteer to walk and play with a neighbor's dog or to feed an animal that's kept in your science room at school. If you like the experience and stick with it for more than a week or two, put some more thought into getting a pet of your own.

Mostly c's

If you really want something cute to cuddle and name, you should probably stick with stuffed animals for now. Read up on pet care and training, and spend time with a friend's or neighbor's pet.

Food for Thought

Do your manners **shine** at **dinnertime,** or do they need **polish?** Take this quiz to find out.

1. The turkey's carved, and you get your plate first. It smells great, and you can hardly wait to dig in. You . . .

a. dig in! After all, you don't want the food to get cold.

b. wait until everybody else has been served and the hostess takes a bite before you dig in.

c. take little nibbles when you think nobody is looking.

2. Oh, no! There's a UFO on your plate—an Unidentified Food Object. You . . .

a. say, "I'm not eating that."

b. take a tiny taste to see if you like it.

c. hide it under some turkey skin.

3. Leave it to Aunt Beth to be fancy. There are three forks at your place. Three?! Which one should you use first?

a. Watch and see which one the hostess uses, and use the same one.

b. Ask. There's no such thing as a dumb question, right?

c. Start with the outside one first.

4. You wanted to sit next to Cousin Wendy. Instead, you're sitting by Granny Smith. "Hello, sweet pea," she says. "How's school?" You . . .

a. say "Fine!" while looking around to see where Cousin Wendy is sitting.

b. pretend you didn't hear her and make an igloo out of your mashed potatoes.

c. tell Granny all about your art project. Then you ask her about her new glasses.

5. From the end of the table, your dad says, "Please pass the peas." They're sitting in front of you. So you . . .

a. pass the peas to the right.

b. pass the peas to the left.

c. scoop up some peas and say, "Please pass your plate, Dad."

6. Halfway through the meal you notice that Aunt Shannon has a glob of cranberry stuck in her teeth. You . . .

a. catch her eye and make a little motion with your hand by your mouth to let her know.

b. say, "Hey, Shannon. You've got something stuck in your teeth!"

c. do nothing. You don't want to embarrass her!

7. Uncle Andrew is telling you a long story when you realize you really, really have to go to the bathroom. You . . .

a. say, "Was that a knock at the door?" and run from the table.

b. sit there until you think you're going to explode, because it's rude to interrupt.

c. say, "Excuse me, Uncle Andrew." Then ask the hostess, "May I be excused for a moment, please?"

Answers

1. The answer is **b.** It's not polite to eat in front of somebody who doesn't have any food. Why? Because watching you eat makes that person hungrier. The hostess is in charge of making sure everybody is served. Then she'll begin eating—and so can you.

2. The answer is **b.** If somebody puts something new on your plate, you should give it a try. Hiding it fools no one, and telling the cook you don't like the looks of it is just as rude.

3. The answers are **a, b,** and **c.** They're all right! Whenever you aren't sure what to do, ask someone or just wait and see what the hostess does. But there's also a nifty secret to every fancy place setting: the silverware for the food that's served first is placed farthest from the plate.

4. The answer is **c.** Conversation is the most important part of a meal, so don't clam up just because you aren't sitting next to your favorite relative. Be friendly! Ask some questions. You and Granny will never get to know each other if you don't give good conversation a chance.

5. The answer is **a.** Pass food, not plates. Food is passed to the right. If you send something the wrong way, two platters are going to end up nose to nose. If it's a big dish, help the next person by holding it while she serves herself.

6. The answer is **a.** If you tell the whole table that Shannon's got a glob in her teeth, she will be embarrassed. But letting her go through the whole meal with that glob will probably embarrass her more. The kindest thing is to let her know in a private way that she needs to clean her teeth.

7. The answer is **c.** There are times when it's O.K. to interrupt an adult if you do so nicely, and this is one of those times. Most adults will understand what you're thinking, and you can slip away without any fuss.

Starring You!

What do your **dreams** of **fame** and **fortune** say about you?
To find out, draw a star around the letter of the answer you choose.

1. Which of these TV shows would you want to star in?

a. a drama about doctors working in a hospital

b. a celebrity talk show

c. a mystery detective drama

d. a sitcom about a large, lovable family

e. a show featuring strange sights and amazing events

2. If someone were to write your life story, what would you want the title to be?

a. **Play to Win**

b. Life of the Party

c. I Did It My Way

d. Home Is Where the Heart Is

e. A Whole World to Explore

3. Which superhero would you most like to be?

a. Major Miracle

She saves a hundred lives in less than an hour with her strength, speed, and problem-solving power.

c. Cyber Saver

She works alone to capture criminals online in electric webs of her own design.

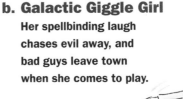

b. Galactic Giggle Girl

Her spellbinding laugh chases evil away, and bad guys leave town when she comes to play.

d. Princess Angel

She's always close by and knows just what you need. There isn't any mind that she can't read.

e. Alexis the Adventurer

She can fly anyplace and visit any time to satisfy her curiosity or to stop a crime.

4. Picture yourself on the cover of a magazine. Which one of these do you think it would be?

a. **Success**   b. **Celebrity Scene**   c. **Art Smart**   d. **Family Crafts**   e. **Young Discoverers**

5. Which award would you most like to win?

a. an Olympic gold medal

b. a Grammy Award for Best Pop Singer

c. the National Award for Best Newspaper Photographer

d. the President's Medal for Teacher of the Year

e. NASA's Most Successful Space Shuttle Pilot Award

6. If an article about you appeared in the paper someday, what would you want the headline to read?

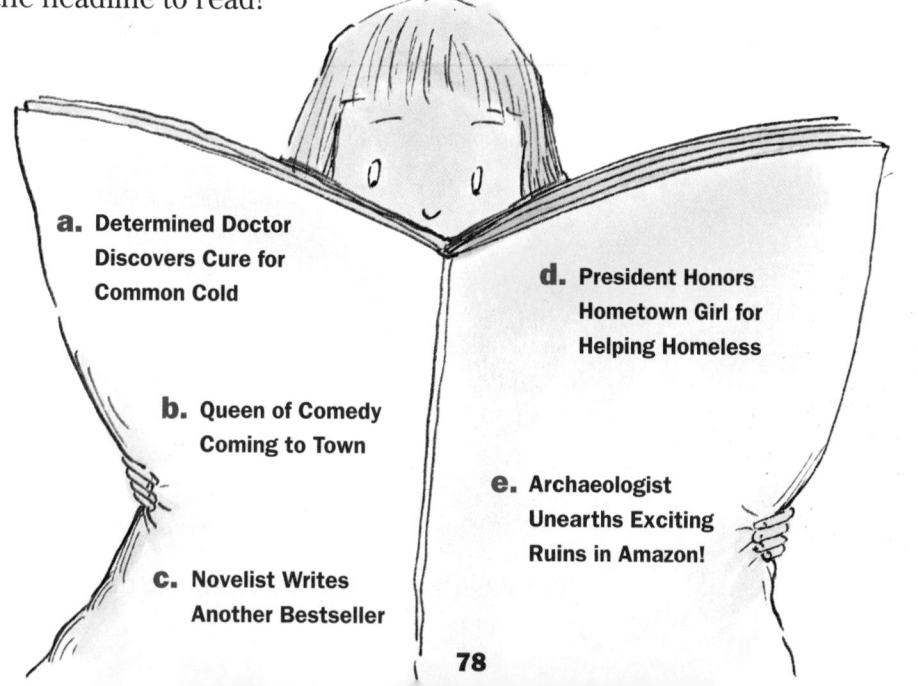

a. Determined Doctor Discovers Cure for Common Cold

b. Queen of Comedy Coming to Town

c. Novelist Writes Another Bestseller

d. President Honors Hometown Girl for Helping Homeless

e. Archaeologist Unearths Exciting Ruins in Amazon!

Answers

Mostly a's

You're a practical girl who's willing to work hard and compete. When you aim for a goal, you're tough to beat!

Mostly b's

You're a fun-loving girl who's warm and carefree. You love company. You like studying with buddies, eating fun snacks, and dancing to your favorite music.

Mostly c's

You're the independent kind with an imaginative mind—a girl who likes to create. You have a style all your own, and you work well alone.

Mostly d's

You have a thoughtful mind and a kind heart. You stick close to home, and you treasure your family and friends above other things. You may dream of being a teacher, a nurse, or another professional who cares for people.

Mostly e's

The sky's the limit for you. You thrive on adventures and look for new things to do. You like to be free to wander and to see whether your dreams can come true.

What did you like best about *The Quiz Book?*

b. revealing answers

a. funny questions

c. kooky pictures

Let us know what you think! Write to:

Quiz Book Editor
Pleasant Company Publications
8400 Fairway Place, P.O. Box 620998
Middleton, Wisconsin 53562

Or visit our Web site:

www.americangirl.com

Published by Pleasant Company Publications
©1999 by Pleasant Company

Printed in Hong Kong. Assembled in China.

00 01 02 03 04 05 06 C&C 10 9 8 7 6 5 4 3 2

American Girl Library® is a registered trademark of Pleasant Company.

Editorial Development: Julie Williams, Michelle Watkins
Art Direction and Design: Chris Lorette David
Cover Art Direction and Design: Kym Abrams, Jean Fujita
Quiz Development: Jordan Jacobowitz, Ph.D, Christine DeCassis, Sidonie DeCassis

Some quizzes in this book have previously appeared in *American Girl*® magazine.

Library of Congress
Cataloging-in-Publication Data
Allen, Laura
The quiz book : clues to you and your friends, too! / by Laura Allen ; illustrated by Debbie Tilley.
p. cm. "American Girl Library."
Summary: Quizzes, questions, and activities for girls to foster self-discovery in
such areas as personal style, friendship, and life skills.
ISBN 1-56247-750-1
1. Girls—United States—Life skills guides Juvenile literature.
2. Girls—United States—Conduct of life Juvenile literature. [1. Life skills. 2. Conduct of life.]
I. Tilley, Debbie, ill. II. American Girl (Middleton, Wis.) III. Title
HQ777.A675 1999 305.23—dc21 99-17482 CIP